The Crystal Cathedral Organ Collection

Twelve Pieces for the Hazel Wright Organ

by ROBERT HEBBLE

Editor: Dale Tucker
Cover Photography: Guy F. Henderson

© 1995 WARNER BROS. PUBLICATIONS INC.
All Rights Reserved

The Hazel Wright Organ

Large by any standard, the Hazel Wright Organ has 13,029 pipes, 223 ranks, 13 divisions, and an ultra modern console with five keyboards. It was acquired in three increments: 94 ranks were completed by Fratelli Ruffatti in 1977 for the former sanctuary, in memory of Dr. and Mrs. Henry Poppen; 100 ranks built by AEolian-Skinner of Boston and installed in 1962 at the Lincoln Center for the Performing Arts in New York City were purchased by Garden Grove Community Church in 1976; and 29 new ranks were added by Ruffatti for the Cathedral installation. The twenty-one rank Antiphonal portion of the 1977 Ruffatti organ remains in the Arboretum.

In 1961, Robert Schuller and the young Garden Grove Community Church opened their first "permanent" sanctuary with a new three manual, 23 rank pipe organ. The brilliant virtuoso concert organist, Virgil Fox, performed the inaugural concert, and this first meeting of Robert Schuller and Virgil Fox would have a tremendous impact on the Crystal Cathedral ministry twenty years later.

In the late sixties, plans for a new, larger organ were discussed with several U.S. and European builders. Eventually, a preference for the work of the Padua, Italy firm owned and operated by Antonio, Francesco, and Piero Ruffatti emerged. In 1972, Dr. Schuller approved a contract for a large 116 rank, five manual organ. When it was inaugurated on April 1st, 1977, the artist was, once again, Virgil Fox.

When architect Philip Johnson produced a small glass model of the proposed Crystal cathedral, immediate questions arose regarding the organ. If it were transferred to the Cathedral, would the new Ruffatti organ be large enough? Inasmuch as large costs and difficult architectural preparations were involved, Dr. Schuller understandably wanted the reassurance of the finest consultation available. He went to Virgil Fox, who accepted his invitation to become consultant and designer of the Crystal Cathedral Organ.

Virgil made a memorable appearance on the "Hour of Power" in November, 1978, and shared his dream of a magnificent Cathedral organ. His dream, however, of inaugurating the third pipe organ in the history of the Robert Schuller ministries was not to be, as it soon developed that Virgil was engaged in a valiant struggle with terminal cancer. He died on October 25th, 1980, but his physicians maintained that his determination to play the Crystal Cathedral Organ actually prolonged his life.

With the purchase of the Lincoln Center AEolian-Skinner in 1976, the church owned two organs of about 100 ranks each. Both had fine pedigrees. Virgil Fox believed that they should be redesigned into one large instrument with extensive additions to the 194 ranks already owned. There was sufficient space in the front of the Cathedral, but the structural engineers had determined a 45 ton limit for the organ and its enclosures. As the organ(s) exceeded 45 tons, Virgil had to assign four divisions to the south balcony. The front organ finally included 173 ranks (much more than the 100 it would have had without Virgil's guidance); the south balcony "Antiphonal" divisions, 43 ranks; the east balcony, 3 ranks (fanfare trumpets); and the west balcony, 4 ranks (fanfare trumpets), all of which add up to 223 ranks. The greatly enlarged front organ is perhaps Virgil's greatest imprint on the project. It required the total assimilation of the AEolian-skinner by Fratelli Ruffatti. The finished organ fully deserved its Fratelli Ruffatti nameplate.

Virgil Fox also designed a console large enough for the combined organs plus the additions. Understandably, our beautiful new console is quite reminiscent of the one he designed for his beloved AEolian-Skinner organ at the Riverside Church in New York City.

Virgil had completed nearly all of the Cathedral organ design at the time of his death. There remained only the execution and oversight of his master plan. This has been expertly carried out by his close friend and protege, Ted Alan Worth. The Crystal Cathedral is deeply indebted to Ted for his devotion, skill, and fidelity to Virgil Fox's dream.

Richard Unfreid

The Hazel Wright Organ - 1995

Significant changes have taken place in the Cathedral organ since Richard Unfreid wrote the fine account of its evolution on the preceding page.

The organ had been in use for only several weeks when I presented the first solo recital upon it, and was subsequently appointed Director of Music and Organist. After living with the instrument for a few months it became obvious that, although it was potentially one of the greatest organs in the world, the extreme pressures of the installation and other factors had left the organ in an unfinished condition both tonally and mechanically. Additionally, it could be heard that the "marriage" of the two instruments, although successful, needed considerable refinement. To accomplish this, work was begun in 1983 and continued through nearly 10 years of loving and careful tonal finishing of the two instruments both to each other and to their new acoustical environment. Together the two represented an immense and colorful stop list - but there were too many duplications of certain stops *and* too many omissions in the tonal spectrum to allow the organ to be as effective as it could be. In order for the dream of Virgil Fox to be fully realized, changes needed to be made.

To that end many stops were revoiced, some ranks were replaced, and a number of additions were made. Throughout the process we have been careful to preserve the integrity of both the AEolian-Skinner and the Ruffatti organs. The organs have been enhanced individually and collectively, and, with the additions, now form a convincing union. Constant maintenance and refinement by an excellent staff of curators continues to assure that his magnificent instrument will maintain its place in the top handful of greatest, as well as largest, in the world. There are now 287 ranks and over 16,000 pipes, plus preparations. The 52 cast bell carillon may be played from each console, as well as mechanically in the tower erected in 1990.

Because of the two world-famous pageants held in the Cathedral - THE GLORY OF CHRISTMAS, and THE GLORY OF EASTER, the choir must be relocated from the front of the church to the rear gallery approximately 5 months of every year. This has necessitated the considerable enlargement of the Gallery organ and the addition of a five-manual console in the Gallery. This console, installed in 1990, controls, as does the main console (which is removed during the pageant runs), the entire resources of the organ. In 1993 the main console was upgraded with new stop jambs and solid state combination action to assist in controlling the many changes and additions made to the organ since its 1982 installation.

Frederick Swann

Dear Friends:

I was a young seminary student preparing to enter the ministry as a bachelor until one weekend when I, as a visiting ministerial student, met a beautiful young organist maned Arvella DeHaan. We met briefly, planned the church service together, and fell in love. So our love, our marriage, and our team partnership in ministry goes back to the pipe organ in the country church in Newkirk, Iowa.

When we were called to begin this church in 1955, I agreed on the condition that I could have, "at least an organ". So we took the $400 farewell gift from our previous church and used it as a down payment on a small electronic organ. My wife became this church's first organist and continued in that role for many years. It was her strong, positive, inspirationally aggressive pressure that lifted my sights until we replaced the electronic organ with our first pipe organ. That was in 1961. When our sanctuary was enlarged, she was the one that finally enabled me to catch the vision for a larger pipe organ to fill the larger auditorium. So, in 1968, through her dynamic faith, we brought the 7,000 pipe Ruffatti organ to Garden Grove.

And again it was Arvella who opened my ears to listen to Virgil Fox who said to me, "Dr. Schuller, I see you are building a Crystal Cathedral!!! That means a larger instrument than what we just finished a few years ago. Let me design it for you".

Even as I pay loving tribute to Hazel Wright, without whom this dream would never have come true, I must thank God for giving me the kind of a wife who gave me the kind of a dream for the organ that sings this weekend for the first time.

No pipe organ has ever been heard by an audience as large as that which will listen to the Hazel Wright Organ. For as we dedicate this organ today, this Crystal Cathedral Congregation commands—by an enormously wide margin—the largest television audience in America of any televised church service. Millions of people in this country and worldwide will enjoy this great organ! When we divide the investment by the people who can enjoy it, it becomes an inexpensive and incredibly beautiful gift to the people of this world.

My final thanks are offered today to the congregation of the Crystal Cathedral. For, in accepting this gift, you are accepting the responsibility to continue to maintain the excellent and high standards established in this Crystal Cathedral.

Together, we will make beautiful music for God!

In His happy service,

Robert H. Schuller

Robert H. Schuller

About The Composer

ROBERT HEBBLE is a composer and organist of international renown. A graduate of Yale University and the Juilliard School, Robert studied with such musical giants as Vittorio Gianinni and Roger Sessions. At Nadia Boulanger's request, he went to Paris to spend a full year of private study in composition and organ with the legendary musician. For over thirty years, Hebble's career was closely linked with the great organist Virgil Fox. Dr. Fox was one of the first to recognize his creative gifts, appointing Hebble as his assistant at the age of sixteen at New York's Riverside Church. Hebble travels extensively as an organist, pianist, composer and clinician throughout the United States, Canada, and Far East. Among many choral and organ commissions, his extensive published writings include the dedicatory organ composition *Heraldings* for the Crystal Cathedral; *Hoc Dies Resurgam* to inaugurate the "Trumpeta Majestatis" organ stop at New York's Riverside Church, and a major work, *A Symphony of Light*, as the premier organ composition commissioned in memory of Virgil Fox which he recently performed in Paris at the Cathedral of Notre Dame.

Throughout his career Robert Hebble has distinguished himself as a colorist; a musician whose conception of beauty finds variety in musical sounds and harmonies the way an artist mixed colors. His prismatic use of musical sounds are the trademark of his concerts, writings and improvisations.

Commissioned by The Crystal Cathedral, Garden Grove, California as the premiere work for the new
Hazel Wright Organ built by Fratelli Ruffatti of Padua, Italy, May, 1982
Dedicated to Dr. and Mrs. Robert H. Schuller

HERALDINGS

SW: Trumpet 8'
GT: Full
CH: Trompette-en-Chamade 8'
PED: Full

ROBERT HEBBLE

8

Swell : Foundations
Great : Full, **Sw.** to **Gt.** 8', 4'
Choir : Trompette-en-Chamade
Pedal : Full, **Sw.** to **Ped.** 8'

Allegro Moderato (♩. = ca. **112**)

sempre staccato

Add **Gt.** to **Ped.** 8'

PSALM PRELUDE

SW: Flutes & Strings 8', 4', tremolo
GT: Principal 8', Flutes 8', 4', Sw. & Ch. to Gt. 8', 4'
CH: Celeste 8', Flutes 8', 4', Sw. to Ch. 8', 4'
PED: Soft 32', 16', 8', Ch. to Ped.

Andante Pastorale (♩ = c. 76)

ROBERT HEBBLE

For Ted Alan Worth

PASTEL

Comb. 1:   SW: Flute 8′, tremolo
             GT: Light Foundations 8′, 4′, 2′, Sw. & Ch. to Gt. 8′, 4′
             CH: Strings 8′, Flutes 8′, 4′, Sw. to Ch. 8′, 4′
             PED: Soft 32′, 16′, 8′, Sw. & Ch. to Ped.

Comb. 2:   SW: Flute Celeste 8′, Flute 8′, tremolo, Sw. to Sw. 4′
             CH: Krummhorn 8′, tremolo
             PED: Soft 16′, 8′, Sw. to Ped.

ROBERT HEBBLE

SW: Fl. Cel. 8', Vox Hum. 8', trem.
GT: Flutes 8', 4'
CH: Flutes 8', 1'

Tempo de Scherzo

PED: Soft 16', 8'

20

DIPTYCH
Based on "Orientis Partibus"

SW: String Celeste 8'
GT: Flute 8'
CH: Krummhorn 8'
PED: Soft 16', 8', Sw. to Ped. 8'

French, ca. 1210
ROBERT HEBBLE

poco rall.

Gt.

Sw.

Gt.

mp

p

pp

Add Soft 32'

SCHEMATICS
Based on "Ton y botel" and "Ebenezer"

SW:
GT: All Foundations, Manuals coupled
CH:
PED:

ROBERT HEBBLE

SOFT STILLNESS AND THE NIGHT

Here we will sit and let the sounds of music creep in our ears -
Soft stillness and the night becomes the touches of sweet harmony.
- The Merchant Of Venice

Comb. 1: SW: Flute Celeste 8', Tremolo, Sw. to Sw. 4'
GT: Flute 4', Tremolo
CH: Gedeckt 8', Tremolo
PED: Gt. to Ped. 8'

Comb. 2: SW: Celeste 8', Vox Humana 8', Tremolo
GT: Principals & Flutes 8', 4', 2'
CH: Celestes 8', Ch. to Ch. 4', Sw. to Ch. 8', 4'
PED: Foundations 32', 16', 8', 4', Sw. & Ch. to Ped. 8', 4',
Gt. to Ped. 8'

ROBERT HEBBLE

To Dr. Jack W. Jones

Meditation on
"MY SHEPHERD WILL SUPPLY MY NEED"
("Resignation")

I: Solo Stop
II: Accompaniment
PED: Bourdons 16', 8', II to Ped. 8'

ROBERT HEBBLE

Commissioned by St. Paul Lutheran Church, Orlando, Florida
Dedicated to Keith E. Bailey

Toccata on "OLD HUNDREDTH"

SW: Trumpet 8'
GT: Foundations 8', 4'
CH: Trompette en Chamade 8'
PED: Foundations 32', 16', 8', 4'

ROBERT HEBBLE

42

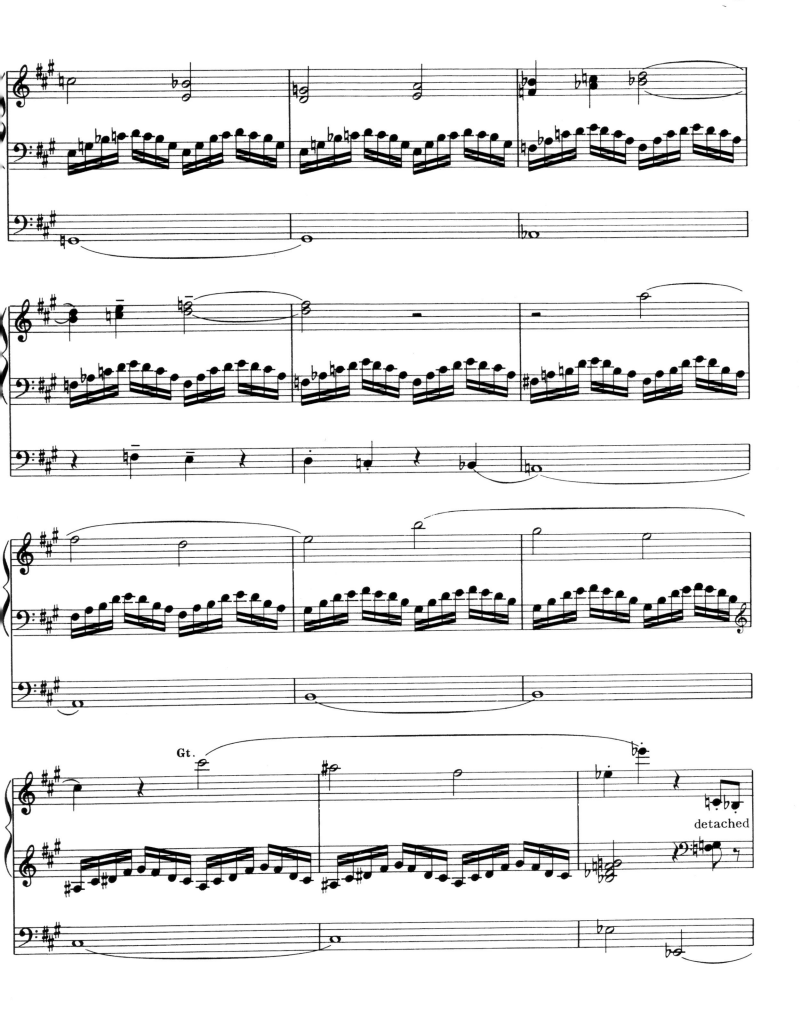

To Virgil Fox
NAVE
Based on "Divinum Mysterium"

SOLO: Gamba Celeste 8'
SW: Flute Celeste 8', Sw. to Sw. 16'
GT: Flute 8'
CH: Strings & Flutes 8', 4', Sw. to Ch. 8', 4'
PED: Bourdon 8', Sw., Ch. & Solo to Ped. 8'

ROBERT HEBBLE

Very slowly and freely (♩ = ♩ throughout)

Ch. { Strings
8', 4', only

Off English Horn
Add Solo Flute 8'

8va - - - - - - - - - - - - - - - - -

Ch. Erzählar
Céleste 8' only

p molto ritard.

a tempo

ritard.

Off Flute 8'
Add Solo French Horn 8'

Off Solo to Ped. 4'
Add Sw. to Ped. 4'

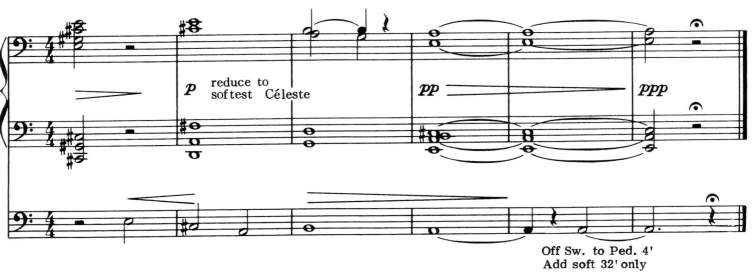

p reduce to
softest Céleste

pp

ppp

Off Sw. to Ped. 4'
Add soft 32' only

Prelude on
"I WONDER AS I WANDER"

Comb. 1:	SW:	Oboe 8'
	GT:	Bourdon 8'
	CH:	Celestes 8', Ch. to Ch. 4'
	PED:	Soft 16', 8', Ch to Ped. 8'

Comb. 2:	SW:	Flutes 8', 4'
	GT:	Bourdon 8'
	CH:	Krummhorn 8',
	PED:	Ch. to Ped. 4' only

Comb. 3:	SW:	
	GT:	Full except Solo Reeds
	CH:	Manuals coupled
	PED:	Foundations 32', 16', 8', 4', Mans. to Ped.

ROBERT HEBBLE

54

SEVEN PALETTE SKETCHES OF UTRILLO
I. Rue des Saints-Pères

SOLO: French Horn 8'
SW: Celestes 8', Flute 8', Tremolo
GT: Flutes 8', 4', Sw. to Gt. 8', 4', Ch. to Gt. 8'
PED: Soft 16', 8', Sw. to Ped.

ROBERT HEBBLE

58

II. Lapin agile sous la neige

I: Flute 8′, Nazard 2-2/3
II: Flute 8′, 4′

59

III. L'église Saint-Séverin

SW: Flute Celeste 8' (Sw. to Sw. 4')
GT: Bourdon 8'
CH: Unda Maris 8', Flute 8', Tremolo
PED: Soft 16', 8', Ch. to Ped. 8'

IV. Paris, vu du Square Saint-Antoine

I: Solo Stop
II: Balanced Accompaniment
PED: Soft 16′, 8′

63

V. L'église Boissy-Saint-Antoine

SW: Oboe 8'
GT: Bourdon 8'
CH: Unda Maris 8', Tremolo
PED: Soft 16', 8', Ch. to Ped. 8'

65

VI. La chapelle de Beaulieu

I: Foundations **mf**
II: Foundations **mp**
PED: Foundations 32′, 16′, 8′, II to Ped.

VII. Crépescule, Golfe du Morbihan

SW: Voix Celeste 8′
GT: Soft Flute 8′
CH: Unda Maris 8′
PED: Soft 16′, 8′, Sw. to Ped. 8′

CELEBRATION

SW: Foundations
GT: Foundations
CH: Trompette-en-Chamade
PED: Full without Reeds

ROBERT HEBBLE